Adrian and Super-A Get Dressed and Say No Way
Text and Illustrations © Jessica Jensen and Be My Rails Publishing 2014
Pictograms kindly provided by www.sclera.be
All Rights Reserved. The only exception is copying the final page(s) intended to be cut out
– limited to purchasers of this book and for personal use only.
ISBN 978-91-982248-1-8

Be My Rails
PUBLISHING

www.BeMyRails.com

Adrian and Super-A

Get Dressed and Say No Way
by Jessica Jensen

Be My Rails

Point at the pictures while reading.

Adjust the story to your child's age and abilities. For a shorter and simpler version of the book — skip some or all of the text in italics.

Let the child point too.

Give a thumbs up or down together.

Little Miss Trigger is a friend you will have to keep an eye on! She is fun ... and very resourceful.

Follow Raily the Train. When Raily has filled each wagon with a picture, he can puff away and rest.

Thummie the Thumb shows us what is right and wrong. Can you give a thumbs up? And a thumbs down?

Adrian is the big brother. He is good at counting, and he can take off his coat and hang it up all by himself.

Super-A can fly and read. Her super powers are: super hearing, super vision, and a super memory.

Their Little Brother mostly crawls around. He eats and poops and has to be allowed to nap.

Get Ready

This is Super-A. She can fly faster than a train!

Super-A is a bit like you and me. At bedtime she cuddles up next to Mom. Mom reads and Super-A listens. Reading is Super-A's favorite thing in the world. Super-A loves looking at the pictures in the books. But she hates to draw! The pictures she likes the most are those in bright colors. Just like her yellow dress.

Super-A loves yellow. She also likes black. The cloak that can make Super-A fly is black! Sometimes Mom and Dad want Super-A to wear another color. This makes Super-A angry. No way will she get dressed then!

☛ *Do you like yellow or not? Point to a big smiley.*
What is your favorite color?

This is Super-A's brother Adrian. He likes everything blue. He does not like yellow at all. Adrian actually thinks yellow is an ugly color.

But when he says that, Super-A gets really upset: "No way is yellow ugly! Yellow is the bestest color in the world!" At least that is what Super-A thinks.

Thummie the Thumb says it is okay to like different colors. Everybody is different. Everybody likes different things.

This is what their little friend Thummie the Thumb will say:

I like one — you like two.
I like black — you like blue.
I like this — you like that.
But you like me and I like you!

FIRST

THEN

It is early in the morning and today Super-A has a plan.

"Let's go outside and play!" Super-A can hardly wait. She starts flitting up and down.

"Yes! I want to go outside too!" Adrian thinks it is a good plan. He does not like yellow, but he sure likes to play outside with Super-A.

"But wait...." Thummie the Thumb looks at Adrian and Super-A. "Isn't there something you forgot to do?"

Adrian and Super-A still have their pajamas on. No way can you go out in your pajamas! People would think you are going to bed. And your pajamas would get dirty!

So what do Adrian and Super-A need to do first?

First, Adrian and Super-A have to get out of their pajamas! They need to get dressed.

☞   First ... get dressed. Then ... go out.

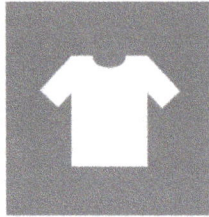

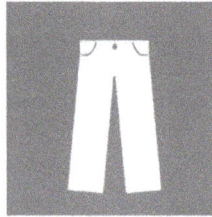

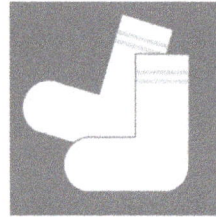

Adrian knows how to put on his clothes. He can do it on his own! Adrian has a shelf in the bathroom. There is a picture of Adrian on it. Super-A has a shelf with a picture too. This is where Mom always puts today's clothes.

Adrian looks at the clothes. He needs to put on the white briefs first. Then a T-shirt and a pair of jeans. And last ... his gray socks.

Mom always prepares two T-shirts for Adrian. Then he gets to pick one. He likes that. But today there is one green and one red.

Adrian is getting upset ... can you guess why?

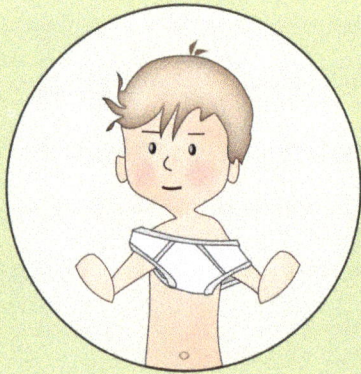

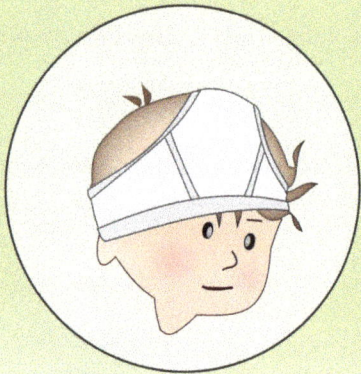

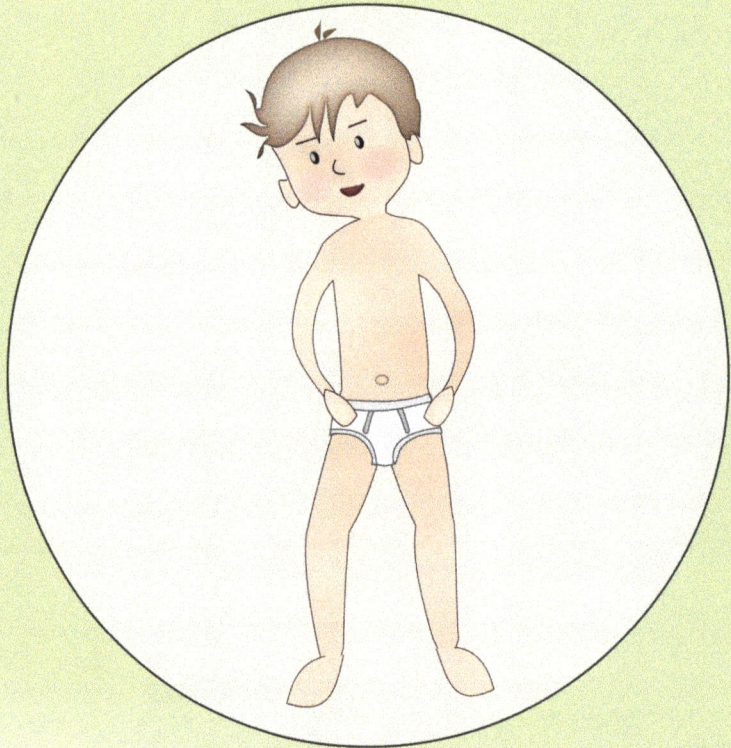

It looks like Adrian could use some help getting dressed today. Let's help him out.

☞ Should Adrian put the briefs on his head?
No, thumbs ... down! Way wacky.

What if he puts his arms through them instead?
No, thumbs ... down!

Should Adrian pull the briefs up over his legs?
Yes! Thumbs ... up!

Adrian knows that underwear is a good thing. You should change your underwear every day. Otherwise, pee and invisible bacterial badness will make you smelly and itchy. Thumbs down!

Adrian wants his blue T-shirt today — the one he had on yesterday! But look! That T-shirt has ketchup on it. Adrian gets angry.

He wants the blue one, not the green T-shirt. And no way does he want the red new one!
"If I cannot have my favorite blue, then I won't wear anything!"
Adrian is upset and he does not want to get dressed at all.

"Oh boy," says Thummie the Thumb. "It's time for the Change Tracks-cap!"
Adrian needs to rethink. Raily the Train comes to help. Adrian cannot have the blue T-shirt, that track is closed. What then? Adrian has to change tracks. He picks the new red T-shirt. Thumbs up! Adrian changed his mind.

"Do you want me to cut off the tag?" Daddy asks.
Adrian nods. No scratchy tag in the neck. That is how he wants it.
He is not upset anymore.

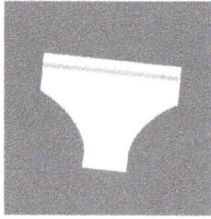

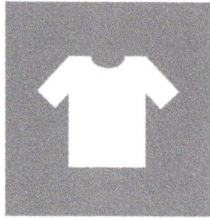

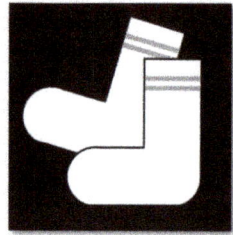

Dad has cut off the tag. Next, Adrian puts on his jeans. Now, where are the socks? They were just here.... Can you see them?

Little Brother has put them on his ears. But that is not where socks should go! Where do socks go?

The socks hurt Adrian's feet. The threads inside are rubbing his toes and choking his ankles. So Dad turns the socks inside out. Guess today will just be one of those inside-out-days for Adrian.

Adrian looks nice and clean in his red T-shirt. Thummie the Thumb agrees ... and do you have your thumbs ready?

> **Nice and clean — gets thumbs ... up!**
> **Nice and clean — gets thumbs ... up!**
> **Dirty clothes — gets thumbs ... down!**
> **Nice and clean — gets thumbs ... up!**

Adrian looks at the blue T-shirt. He can see how dirty it is. It should go into the laundry hamper. That is where dirty clothes go.

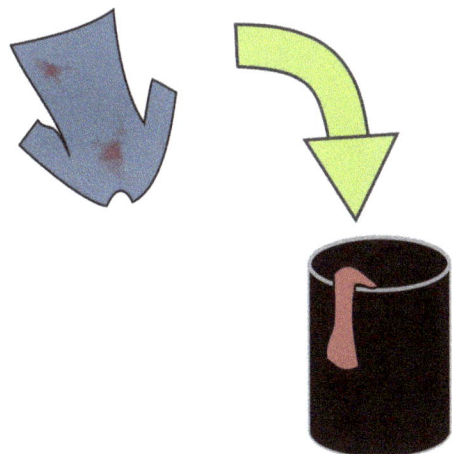

Super-A always wears yellow. But today there isn't a yellow dress on the shelf. Today there is a red dress. And that dress is for parties! Dad knows that Super-A will only wear yellow. He looks around. Little Miss Trigger seems to know a thing or two about the yellow dress.

But ... where is Super-A? Super-A is flying everywhere. Over the shower head and around the shampoos.

"Super-A! Come down to your yellow dot!" Dad points to the yellow dot on the floor. It is a special dot. Super-A's very own special dot. That is where Super-A stands to get dressed every morning.

Dad is waiting for her. But Super-A forgets to listen to Dad. She forgets she wants to go out and play. Super-A forgets all about getting dressed.

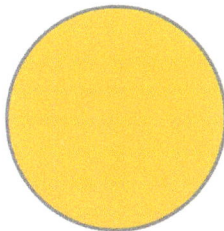

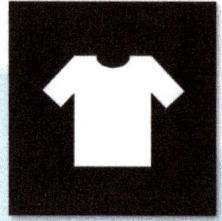

Suddenly Super-A remembers what Thummie the Thumb always says. Are you ready?

Still on dot — gets thumbs ... up!
Still on dot — gets thumbs ... up!
Twist and twirl — gets thumbs ... down!
Still on dot — gets thumbs ... up!

Super-A puts both her hands up in the air. Daddy pulls the yellow dress over her in just one go. There. Done.

Super-A does not like to brush her hair. But Daddy gives her a sticker each time she does. Her brush is almost full of stickers. And her Mom is happy to see all that pretty hair. Super-A needs to brush her hair or it will get all tangled up. Mom says it will look just like a bird's nest. Super-A does not want birds in her hair.

Super-A brushes her hair. She gets a sticker. Last of all, Super-A gets her black cloak back on.

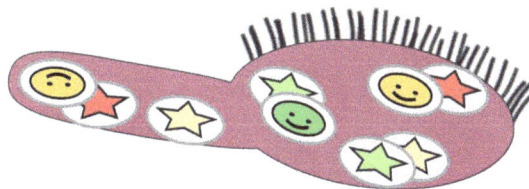

Super-A wants to go outside at once. She is already on her way. "But wait!" Thummie the Thumb knows better. "First ... you need to ask an adult. All children need to ask an adult b-e-f-o-r-e they go out to play."

☞ Super-A wants to go out now. Adrian wants to go out now. But is Mommy okay with that? Let's find out!

Super-A asks. Then she listens to Mom. Mommy says: "No. You have to eat breakfast first!"

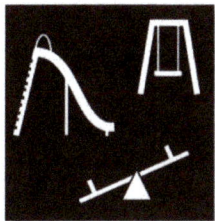

FIRST

THEN

First breakfast. Then go outside.

And Mom is right. Nobody wants to be hungry when they play.

Adrian and Super-A have to change tracks. Going out has to wait! Put on your Change Tracks-caps! It is time to rethink.

So Adrian and Super-A help to set the table. If they all help, then they can have fun faster.

They eat breakfast. Then Mom puts all the food back where it belongs. Some food goes inside the kitchen cabinets. Some food goes into the fridge where it keeps cold and fresh. The kids put away their plates.

Good job helping out! Can you give them a thumbs up?

1   2   3

Fun Outside

Now it is time for today's mission. They are going outside. Raily the Train has three tasks for them. Can you see what he wants Adrian and Super-A to do first?

☞ First ... dress for the weather.
Then ... build a sand castle.
Last ... put away their coats and boots.

Super-A uses her super hearing power. She can hear leaves and rain falling to the ground. Wet leaves and water puddles outside — that means super protective clothes!

Little Miss Trigger thinks they should put on a swimsuit. But let's ask Thummie instead. Ready?

Should they put on a swimsuit? No, thumbs ... down!
Their party clothes? No, thumbs ... down!
Rain boots? Yes, thumbs ... up!
A sun hat? No, thumbs ... down!
Pajamas? No, thumbs ... down! Way wacky.
A raincoat? Yes! Thumbs ... up!

Adrian is quick today. He has already put on his waterproof pants, his raincoat, a warm hat and the blue rain boots.

But it looks like Super-A was in a hurry! What did Super-A forget?

Super-A forgot to put on her raincoat.

So Daddy helps her put it on. He says: "Right hand in … and right hand out. Left hand in … and left hand out."

Now everything they have to wear in the rain is on. Adrian and Super-A are both ready for the weather.

☞ *Watch Raily the Train! He can collect the first picture and put it into his wagon. Just two tasks to go. Raily the Train can move on. Good job, everyone!*

1

2   3

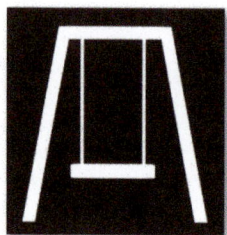

Super-A wants their mom to come to the playground. But Mom has to buy some new winter boots. Someone has to do that too....

Adrian does not want Mom. He wants to bring his bulldozer. "Don't you want a bulldozer too? The yellow one?" Daddy looks at Super-A when he asks her.
"No ... thanks." Super-A shakes her head.
"That's okay," Daddy says, "we don't always want the same."

At the playground Adrian and Super-A take turns deciding. First Super-A picks what to play.

The swings or the slide?
Super-A wants to ride the slide.

It stopped raining, but the slide is wet. It is good luck that they have their super protective clothes on. Now they can ride the slide even if there is rain on it.

But, oh no! Little Miss Trigger forgets to wait until no one is down the slide. Little Miss Trigger almost smashes into Super-A. It is a good thing Super-A is as quick as she is! She flies up and out of the way.

Now Super-A wants them all to swing, but they have to take turns deciding. Whose turn is it?

It is Adrian's turn to decide. Dad looks at Adrian and asks: "What do you want to play?"

☞ Adrian wants to play in the sandbox — Super-A does not. "No way!" Super-A shouts. "I want to swing!"

But when Dad says they can build a large castle made of sand, Super-A is happy again. She rethinks. She forgets all about the swing. Super-A thinks about the sand castle instead! Her mind changes tracks.

Raily the Train is happy too. It is time for the second picture!

☞ Adrian starts filling his blue bucket with sand. Super-A decides to fill her yellow one. Then Dad helps them turn the buckets upside down. They build a castle with four towers.

They also find some stones. Very gently they put the stones on the castle made of sand. They do not want it to break. Adrian finds a leaf. It can be a flag! Adrian puts the brown leaf-flag on top of their castle. Adrian and Super-A look at their castle and they feel proud. But then....

Oh no! Little Miss Trigger says: "No way!" She does not want the flag. Just stones. Little Miss Trigger starts kicking.

Do we want the castle to fall apart?
No, thumbs ... down!

So Dad fixes the hole with some sand. Daddy says that you do not kick and you do not pull someone's hair. You talk instead. Little Miss Trigger and Super-A say sorry. Then Dad builds a new castle for Little Miss Trigger. One without a flag. Now they have two castles. They have finished their second picture. Another task can go into Raily the Train's wagon. Good job, everyone!

2

3

It is Super-A's turn to decide again. She wants them all to swing. It is not Adrian's turn to decide, but he wants to play with his bulldozer. That is something Super-A really does not want to do. Dad says you can do different things. You do not need to do the same things. That way, both get to do what they want.

Adrian starts playing with his bulldozer. He is happy. Super-A goes on the swings. She is happy too! But then Little Miss Trigger writes "Mom" in the sand. And that makes Super-A want to go home.

She misses Mom. Dad says to wait. But Super-A is not in the mood. She wants to go home now. Not soon. Not later. Now!

Adrian wants to play more. He is not done digging. So Mom comes and gets Super-A. Adrian can dig some more.

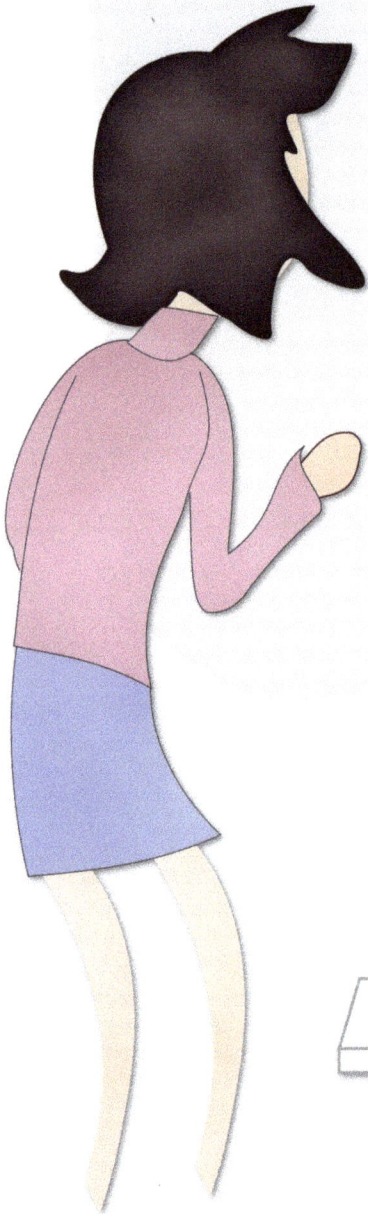

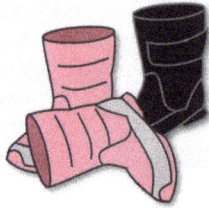

Mom has bought some winter boots. She did that when Super-A was at the playground.

Now there are three new pairs of boots waiting at home. Super-A h-a-t-e-s new shoes, but she does not want somebody else to pick for her. So she tries all of them on. The yellow ones are the prettiest. Her eyes like them. But her feet like to be in the black ones. The black boots squeeze less and the lining is fuzzy and soft. The feet get to pick today!

Mom puts a new yellow dot on the shoe rack. That is where the black new boots will live.

Mom will return the other new boots to the store. The pink and the yellow boots are un-chosen.

Adrian comes inside too. He hangs up his coat and puts the rain boots on the shoe rack. Super-A looks at Raily the Train and she sees her clothes all over the floor.

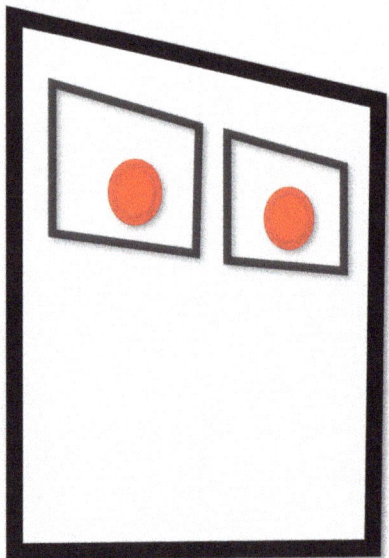

Super-A picks up her rain boots. The rain boots should go on the shoe rack, right next to her new winter boots. She hangs her coat on the hook with the yellow dot. Mission accomplished! Raily the Train has a big smile on his face. They have finished all of their tasks. His wagons are all full!

First they ... got dressed for the weather. Then they ... built a sand castle. And last they ... put away their clothes.

Raily the Train can puff away and rest now! Choo-choo!

But Mom is not done. Mom shows Super-A four completely new dresses. They are all the same. Yellow, just how Super-A likes them. But still — new!
"You can try one on after dinner," Mom says.

Hmm. We will see about that....

Cut out the paper dolls and pictograms. Practice how to get dressed with your child!

1) What should Adrian and Super-A wear inside? And outside in the rain? Let your child dress the paper dolls. Do they like all their clothes?

2) In what order do we put on clothes? Order the pictograms.

3) Where do we keep our clothes? Let your child go on a quest to find each pictogram among his or her own clothes. Place the real clothes on the floor in the right order with a pictogram on top. Leave them out for tomorrow!

4) How does your child feel about the clothes? What colors, textures, or patterns does your child like the most? Is there something about the clothes your child does not like? Why? How do the clothes feel on your body?

Can your child find yours or a sibling's clothes as well? Which are the favorite clothes of friends and family members? Why? Do they like the same things about clothes?

5) What does your child wear in the rain? Give your child one cut-out at a time and have your child show you the raincoat and rain boots.

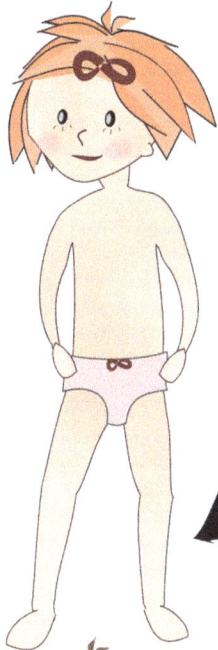

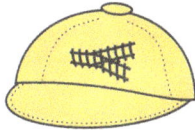

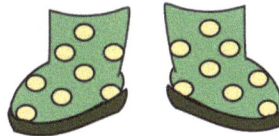

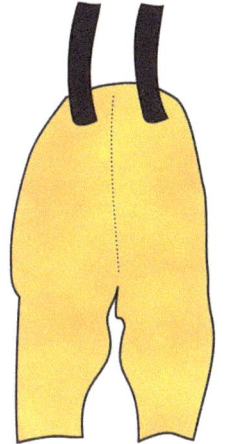

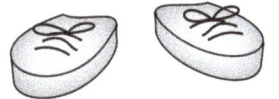

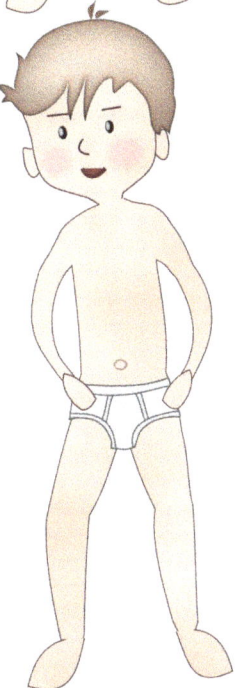

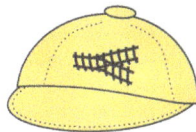

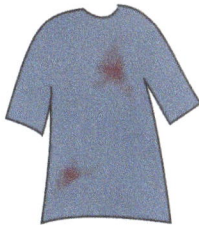

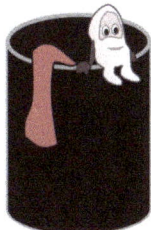

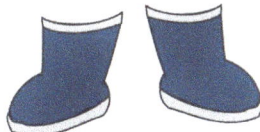